Hispanic Heritage

Hispanic Heritage

Title List

Central American Immigrants to the United States

Refugees from Unrest

by Eric Schwartz

Mason Crest Publishers
Philadelphia

Mason Crest Publishers Inc.

370 Reed Road, Broomall, Pennsylvania 19008

(866) MCP-BOOK (toll free)

www.masoncrest.com

13 12 11 10 09 08 07 06   10 9 8 7 6 5 4 3 2

Library of Congress Cataloging-in-Publication Data

Schwartz, Eric.

  Central American immigrants to the United States : refugees from unrest / by Eric Schwartz.

     p. cm. — (Hispanic heritage)

  Includes bibliographical references and index.

  ISBN 1-59084-929-9—ISBN 1-59084-924-8 (series)

  1. Central American Americans—Social conditions—Juvenile literature. 2. Immigrants—United States—Social conditions—Juvenile literature. 3. Refugees— United States—Social conditions—Juvenile literature. 4. United States—Ethnic relations—Juvenile literature. 5. Central America—Politics and government—1979— Juvenile literature. I. Title. II. Hispanic heritage (Philadelphia, Pa.)

  E184.C34S39 2005

  305.868'728073—dc22

                            2004025134

Produced by Harding House Publishing Service, Inc., Vestal, NY.

www.hardinghousepages.com

Interior design by Dianne Hodack and MK Bassett-Harvey.

Cover design by Dianne Hodack.

Printed in the Hashemite Kingdom of Jordan.

Contents

Introduction

by José E. Limón, Ph.D.

Even before there was a United States, Hispanics were present in what would become this country. Beginning in the sixteenth century, Spanish explorers traversed North America, and their explorations encouraged settlement as early as the sixteenth century in what is now northern New Mexico and Florida, and as late as the mid-eighteenth century in what is now southern Texas and California.

Later, in the nineteenth century, following Spain's gradual withdrawal from the New World, Mexico in particular established its own distinctive presence in what is now the southwestern part of the United States, a presence reinforced in the first half of the twentieth century by substantial immigration from that country. At the close of the nineteenth century, the U.S. war with Spain brought Cuba and Puerto Rico into an interactive relationship with the United States, the latter in a special political and economic affiliation with the United States even as American power influenced the course of almost every other Latin American country.

The books in this series remind us of these historical origins, even as each explores the present reality of different Hispanic groups. Some of these books explore the contemporary social origins—what social scientists call the "push" factors—behind the accelerating Hispanic immigration to America: political instability, economic underdevelopment and crisis, environmental degradation, impoverished or wholly absent educational systems, and other circumstances contribute to many Latin Americans deciding they will be better off in the United States.

And, for the most part, they will be. The vast majority come to work and work very hard, in order to earn better wages than they would back home. They fill significant labor needs in the U.S. economy and contribute to the economy through lower consumer prices and sales taxes.

When they leave their home countries, many immigrants may initially fear that they are leaving behind vital and important aspects of their home cultures: the Spanish language, kinship ties, food, music, folklore, and the arts. But as these books also make clear, culture is a fluid thing, and these native cultures are not only brought to America, they are also replenished in the United States in fascinating and novel ways. These books further suggest to us that Hispanic groups enhance American culture as a whole.

Our country—especially the young, future leaders who will read these books—can only benefit by the fair and full knowledge these authors provide about the socio-historical origins and contemporary cultural manifestations of America's Hispanic heritage.

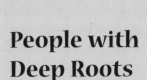

People with Deep Roots

The United States of America is truly a diverse nation. For more than two hundred years, people from all over the world have come to the United States in search of opportunity and a better life. Here, these immigrants have joined together to make a nation like no other. The road has seldom been easy.

Artwork

The chapter openers in this book are based on *molas*, a form of Central American fabric art.

A street mural in California portrays the diversity of immigrants coming to the United States.

oppressed: dominated someone, usually extremely harshly.

exploited: took advantage of someone.

culture: the shared beliefs, customs, practices, and social behavior of a particular nation or people.

Different communities within the United States sometimes clash, and certain groups have *oppressed* and *exploited* others. Today, however, more and more Americans are realizing that each *culture* makes valuable contributions to America, and diversity is one of the greatest gifts the United States can offer to the world.

Despite an increasing appreciation for cultural diversity and the richness it adds to our lives, many Americans still don't know very much about cultures other than their own. Think about it for a moment. How much do you know about Chinese Americans, Irish Americans, Russian Americans, Iranian Americans, Kenyan Americans, Jewish Americans, Christian Americans, or any other group you could possibly mention? Chances are you know quite a bit about groups to which you belong, and maybe you even know a bit about groups that are culturally similar to your own. But there's a whole world of people out there, and each one has valuable stories to tell.

Colorful masks demonstrate the skills of Central Americans.

In the United States, people of Central American descent are considered part of the Latino population. Latinos are now the largest minority group in America, and Central Americans are the fastest-growing sector of the Latino population.

Just as the overall population of the United States is varied, Central American communities are themselves extremely diverse. Central America, the narrow strip of land that links southern Mexico to the South American continent, is made up of seven countries: Belize, Guatemala, Honduras, El Salvador, Nicaragua, Costa Rica, and Panama, and each has its own history and culture. Therefore, before we learn more about the lives of Central American immigrants in the United States, let's take a closer look at the land and history from which these people come.

11

Central Americans are known for their skillful weaving.

Central America: Early History

tectonic plates: sections of the Earth's crust that move and are characterized by volcanic action and earthquake activity.

oughly three million years ago, two of Earth's massive *tectonic plates* collided, and Central America was born. The new land bridged the North and South American continents. Over time, plants, animals, and people flowed over this bridge in a back and forth migration that made Central America

Latino and Hispanic: Terms of Inclusion and Confusion

In the United States today, the term "Latino" is popularly used to refer to any person from Latin America or with Latin American heritage. Technically, however, this is not the proper use of the term. Latino is a linguistic term, meaning it is based on language. A person is considered Latino if she comes from the Americas and has a Spanish, French, or Portuguese (all languages based on Latin) background. People who come from Latin America but do not speak a Latin-based language (for example, people who speak a Native language) are not technically considered Latino.

The term "Hispanic" is similar to Latino in that it also is a linguistic term. A person is considered Hispanic if he comes from the Americas and has a Spanish-speaking background. People who speak French or Portuguese (the main languages of some South American countries) are considered Latino but not Hispanic.

a land of rich diversity. In the midst of this diversity, some of the most highly developed civilizations in the Americas rose.

Where the Native people of the Americas came from is still hotly debated, but the most popular theory is that their ancestors came from Asia over another land bridge, this one near present-day Alaska. *Archaeologists* believe this happened sometime between 40,000 and 10,000 BCE. In the thousands of years that followed, these people would have multiplied, traveled, and spread out until communities lived throughout both American continents.

For centuries, the first inhabitants of the Americas left little record of their presence. They survived by hunting wild animals, gathering plants, and fishing. But around 5000 BCE, the native people started cultivating crops, and life changed enormously. Communities became more settled because they had to stay in one place long enough for the crops to grow. Societies also had to become more organized to successfully farm the land.

Some of the crops grown earliest in Central America were root crops, like sweet potatoes and manioc (another starchy vegetable), which were carried across the land bridge from South America. Three thousand years later, corn came to Central America from the north. Corn had a radical effect on Central American life, and the land's ability to support corn cultivation greatly impacted the types of societies that developed in different Central American regions.

In regions where corn cultivation was impossible because of the rainy climate, people continued to live in independent semi-*nomadic* tribes. They foraged for *sustenance* and traded with the more developed regions of Central America. In the south, where the land could support cornfields for a short time, the people practiced what is called "slash-and-burn" agriculture, cutting

The mountains of Central America

down portions of the forest, burning the area to remove vegetation and put nutrients into the soil, and ultimately abandoning the plots when the soil became exhausted. In these areas, societies were somewhat more organized and were controlled by regional chiefs. In contrast, in the north, where the land was most fertile, people lived in permanent settlements. They built irrigation canals, planted fields, and used advanced cultivation techniques. In these areas, organized civilizations such as the Olmec and Maya developed.

Corn played a vital role in Mayan culture.

y 1000 BCE, corn had become the staple of Central American civilizations and figured prominently in their rituals and creation myths. In Maya mythology, for example, the corn god symbolizes creation and renewal. In the Popol Vuh, the main religious text of the Quiche Maya, the young corn god plays a critical role in the birth of the sun and the creation of the world. According to other Maya legends, humans were formed from cornmeal. To this day, intricate rituals reflecting Maya mythology and worldviews govern corn planting.

The Olmec left huge stone heads as reminders of their culture.

The Rise of Civilizations

he Olmec are often regarded as the founding culture of Mesoamerica, the region that includes modern-day Mexico and most of Central America. On the East Coast, in what is now southeast Mexico, the Olmec had developed a unique civilization by about 1200 BCE. They built one of the first cities in Mesoamerica, now known as San Lorenzo, which sat on a 2,000- by 3,000-feet (609.6m- by 914.4m) man-made platform. At another site, the Olmec constructed what may be the first pyramid in the Americas. They depended on corn for their food, but also traded extensively in commodities such as cocoa beans (the main ingredient of chocolate), jade, obsidian, and animal hides.

The Mayans left behind the ruins of sophisticated architecture.

No one knows exactly what happened to the Olmec. They disappeared into the mists of time, but not before profoundly influencing other cultures in the area. The Mixtec, Aztec, and Maya cultures (just to name a few) all owed a debt to the Olmec. Although politically distinct, artistically diverse, and often warring, these cultures also had many things in common. They were ruled by noble dynasties who were regarded as *divine*. They worshiped their ancestors, a trait that endures among the Native peoples of the region to this day, and their cities—many of which were larger than European cities of the time—were organized around huge public spaces constructed for religious and political rituals.

Of these civilizations, the Maya are considered the most important *pre-Columbian* civilization in Central America. The term "Maya" is broad and encompasses Native peoples who spoke about thirty-one closely related languages and dialects, many of which are still spoken today. Maya *city-states* dominated northern Central America, and their culture extended into the south of the *isthmus*. The Maya civilization was at its height between 250 and 900 CE, called the "Classic Period."

The Maya may be best known for their architectural prowess. Using concrete and limestone, the Maya built large cities that included ritual plazas, ball courts, and sweat baths. Paved roads connected neighborhoods to the city center. Artificial reservoirs held water for irrigating the farms. But the Maya were more than good builders. They were also serious intellectuals. Excellent observers of the night sky, the Maya could calculate the 500-year cycle of Venus within a two-hour margin of error. They used carefully constructed buildings as astronomical tools, and their solar calendar was more accurate than that of the Spanish *conquistadors*. It remains in use in some Maya towns to this day.

The Maya were also great mathematicians and very prolific writers. They were among the first peoples in the world to use the concept of zero, and they painted books upon tree-bark paper and carved texts into stone. In Honduras, for example, artisans carved an entire history of the ruling dynasty into a stone staircase.

No one knows exactly why the Maya civilization declined after the Classic Period, but one theory is that the Maya population grew beyond what the land could sustain. The cities alone had about 50,000 residents, and the area as a whole housed millions of people. Supporting this population resulted in massive deforestation as trees were cut to produce wood, clear farmland, and burn limestone to create the building materials for the cities. There is also evidence that a great drought

divine: from God.

pre-Columbian: before the arrival of Christopher Columbus.

city-states: independent states that consist of self-ruling cities and their surrounding territories.

isthmus: a narrow strip of land that joins two larger land areas.

CE: common era, often used instead of AD.

conquistadors: Spanish explorers or conquerors.

peninsula: a narrow piece of land that projects from the mainland into a body of water.

he Maya used hieroglyphics, a true writing system, rather than the pictographs used by other neighboring cultures. While archaeologists finally deciphered the Maya calendar early in the 20th century, it took nearly one hundred years more before the main texts began to be understood. Archaeologists can now read the detailed histories of dynasties, descriptions of the power struggles of kings, and chronicles of wars between neighboring kingdoms.

hit the area and lasted for more than one hundred years. The ruling class's inability to ease the people's suffering may have led to a general loss of faith in the religion and government, and uprisings may have resulted.

Of course, the Maya culture did not completely disappear. In the highlands of Guatemala and in the northern Yucatan (the Mexican *peninsula* that extends into the Gulf of Mexico), Maya cities continued into what is known as the Post-Classic Mayan period (900–1524 CE), but the urban centers were not as grand

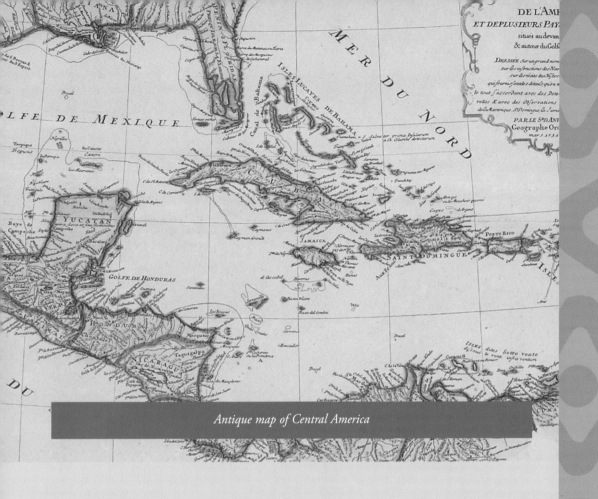

Antique map of Central America

and left fewer written records. By the 1500s, however, Central America was about to change forever, for a new people were landing on its shores.

Central America Conquered

Spanish is the main language spoken today in Central America. But why is Spanish, rather than the language of one of the great civilizations we just discussed, now the leading language of this region's people? The answer lies in the events of the Colonial Era, a time when European powers explored and then conquered lands and peoples, claiming vast riches and natural resources for their empires.

Central America's first contact with the European powers came in 1502 when Christopher Columbus, an Italian explorer working for the Spanish crown, sailed into the Bay of Honduras. The expedition met some Native traders and was surprised by the cotton clothing, stone knives, and copper hatchets the traders carried. The expedition, however, was Columbus's fourth and final voyage to the Americas, and Central America was spared, for a time, further contact with the conquistadors. Then in 1517, Spanish explorer Francisco Hernández de Córdoba sailed along the coast of Yucatan with a shipload of would-be settlers. From their ships, they could see a number of large towns, one so large that they called it "Grand Cairo." One expedition member later described what they had seen:

> They led us to some very large buildings of fine masonry which were the prayer houses of their idols, the walls of which were painted with the figures of great serpents and evil-looking gods. In the middle was something like an altar, covered with clotted blood, and on the other side of the idols were symbols like crosses, and all were colored. We stood astonished, never having seen or heard of such things before.

The news of the mysterious civilization sparked interest among other Spanish explorers and colonists. The gold-hungry Spanish were dissatisfied with the treasure they had found in the Caribbean (where Columbus had landed in 1492), and by 1518 the governor of Cuba had organized a better-equipped expedition to the land of the Maya. It would become a vicious conquest. The Spaniards were excited by the gold jewelry they saw, and the Native traders they encountered pointed to the north, explaining that it came from "Mexico." The explorers followed the directions, continued west, and finally came to the edge of the Aztec Empire, where they found more gold and the Aztecs who had been sent especially to meet them. Another expedition was soon prepared. In 1519 Hernán Cortés set sail with a fleet of ships, sixteen horses, and 508 soldiers. Within two and a half years, the Aztec Empire would be destroyed.

Spanish explorers encountered buildings like this one in Central America.

A carving of a serpent head in the ruins of Teotihuacan

At the time, the Aztecs were the dominant empire of Mesoamerica. Their capital, Tenochtitlan, had a population of almost 250,000, making it one of the largest cities anywhere in the world. Powerful as the Aztecs were, they viewed the encroaching Spaniards with alarm. The great Aztec ruler Montezuma encouraged neighboring tribes to unite against the strange bearded men with their fearsome horses.

The Aztecs, however, had many enemies. They had long conquered other tribes in the area, and now some of those tribes preferred to join Cortés to defeat the Aztecs. Others knew the Spanish must be resisted at all costs and united with their former enemies. The Maya kingdom of Quiche in the highlands of Guatemala had resisted the Aztec expansion years earlier, but they answered Montezuma's call for assistance. But in 1521, Cortés overpowered the Aztecs in the conquest of Tenochtitlan. He obtained the list of tribes that paid *tribute* to Montezuma and contacted each one, demanding they now pay tribute to the Spanish crown. With the Aztecs destroyed, Cortés turned his sights on the rebellious Quiche Maya, and he sent his leading captain, Pedro de Alvarado, a man known both for his loyalty and his brutality, to obtain their allegiance. On December 6, 1523, Alvarado set out on his mission with 400 Spanish soldiers and between 5,000 and 10,000 Native soldiers from conquered tribes and allies.

When he got to Guatemala, Alvarado found more than a third of the Quiche population already dead. A smallpox epidemic (a disease the Spanish had introduced to Central America just a few years earlier) had ripped through the area. Alvarado gave the remaining Quiche a choice: surrender to the Spanish crown or go to war. Despite their much-weakened condition, the Quiche chose war. They sought allies among the neighboring Maya, but as happened with the Aztecs, some of their rivals sided with the Spanish. Although they gathered 10,000 troops, the Quiche were soon defeated, and Alvarado destroyed their capital of Utatlan.

In the years that followed, the Spanish wreaked havoc on Central America. Alvarado organized brutal expeditions to conquer twelve independent Maya kingdoms just within the Guatemalan highlands. The conquistadors tortured the Native people. Their trained dogs tore people's bodies to pieces. Those who survived the battles, diseases, and torture were forced to fight in the Spanish armies. Native chiefs were burned alive, and the Spanish went about erasing the Maya culture by destroying their cities, demolishing artwork, and burning thousands of their books.

tribute: payment by one ruler or state to another.

25

Once the Native people were conquered, they were enslaved. The Spanish shipped thousands of Central Americans to work as slaves in Cuban and Jamaican mines. They shipped thousands more to South America where the Inca Empire was now under attack and its great wealth ravaged. While it's impossible to know for sure, some historians estimate that as many as half a million people from Nicaragua and 150,000 from Honduras were sent as slaves to South America. The conditions were so bad on the slave ships that only one out of five people arrived alive.

The Spanish now claimed complete control of Central America, and they called their new realm the "Kingdom of Guatemala." This "kingdom" stretched from roughly the present-day southern border of Mexico to Panama.

In less than a century, the Native tribes of Central America suffered a fearsome human cost. In 1500, the Native population stood at roughly 5.65 million. Just seventy years later—after the ravages of war, Spanish-introduced diseases, and slavery—approximately 550,000 remained. Nearly five million people had died or been displaced, representing one of the worst population declines in human history.

A New Society

The Spanish conquest of the Americas forever changed the face of Central America. While the conquest was a brutal takeover in which millions of people died, today most Central Americans recognize Spanish ancestry and culture as an important part of their own culture and heritage. White Spanish settlers, although the minority, became an important part of the population, and their religion (Catholicism), art, and customs shaped much of the larger society. Before long, the Spanish population began mixing with the Native population, each adapting to the other.

The Spanish and Native peoples weren't the only ones contributing to Central America's society and culture. People of African descent were also becoming a significant portion of the population. Brought originally to the Kingdom of Guatemala as slaves, the

A modern street mural portrays the oppression of Native people.

he Spanish brutality caused deep resentment among the Native people, and they rebelled regularly. The most famous rebellion was in Honduras, the center of the Caribbean slave trade. Led by Lempira, chief of the Lenca Indians, 200 towns and 30,000 warriors participated in the uprising, which inspired other rebellions in turn. The Spanish assassinated Lempira during peace negotiations, but uprisings continued to plague the Spanish for centuries.

An Empire Built on Their Backs

espite their drastically reduced numbers, the Native peoples of Central America still represented more than 80 percent of the Central American population throughout the 1600s. While they were no longer enslaved (enslavement of the Native peoples had been outlawed in 1542), they were still forced to pay tribute to the Crown, the Catholic Church, and the landed estates created by the original conquistadors. This tribute provided more than 70 percent of the resources for the kingdom. The Native people paid their tribute in the form of products such as wool, cotton, corn, and wheat. These products were auctioned, and the cash went to the Royal Treasury.

African people also contributed to the cultural mix. In Central American society today, you can still identify the Native, Spanish, and African roots in many aspects of the culture.

In the new Central American society, skin color and ancestry determined much about the type of life a person led. There was no such thing as equality. The society became highly *stratified*. Not only were there divisions between the Native, Spanish, and African peoples, there were also divisions within these groups. For example, white Spanish society was separated into two categories: the *Peninsulares* and the *Criolles*. Peninsulares were people who had been born in Spain, and they were at the top of the Central American social pyramid. Criolles were Spanish people who had been born in the New World, and they had lower status than the Peninsulares. People of mixed racial heritage were called *mestizos*, and they too had different categories. For example, *Zambos* were people of mixed African and Native heritage while *Mulattos* were people of mixed African and Spanish heritage. Today, people of mixed racial heritage make up the majority of Central America's population.

Central America's early history and the development of its society eventually led to the events and conditions that caused unrest in the region throughout the nineteenth and twentieth centuries. It is this unrest that would lead so many Central Americans to flee their homes in search of a better life in the United States.

stratified: formed into layers.

Habla Español

historia (ees-tore-ee-ah): history

gente (hane-tay): people

populación (pope-oo-lah-see-own): population

cultura (cool-too-rah): culture

29

2

A Region in Conflict

"My group was then sent to Quiche in 1978, when General Lucas Garcia was elected president. Our orders were to kill whole families. The reason why we killed is that we were told that the Americans wanted more *communists* killed, and if we did that, we would get a salary increase, better food, new shoes, and new helicopters. That was proof to us that the Americans were behind what we were doing."

communists: people who believe in communism, an economic philosophy that believes in a classless society and the ownership and control of wealth and property by the state.

Central America's farmland

"I remember one case where the owner of a coffee plantation had killed the wife of one of the campesinos, who had six children. The owner then went to the man and gave him fifty quetzales to keep his mouth shut. One of the military police went and cut off the campesino's ear and six of his toes. One of my friends then killed the military policeman who did this—and killed the peasant also because he was suffering and dying from the wounds. He put him out of his misery.

"My uncle then killed the six children. My uncle has since become professor of karate and chief of patrols of the National Police. Around the time of the Mejia Victores coup in early August 1983, my uncle massacred two hundred fifty persons in Quiche simply because he wanted their land. He is a wealthy man and a big killer."

—testimony from a former sergeant in the Guatemalan Army

Independence for Central America

n September 15, 1821, Central America won its independence from the Spanish crown, but the people were still not free from hardship. With independence came a whole new era of struggles as leaders fought for control of states and boundaries were established. First, Mexico annexed the region, but its rule lasted only two years. In 1823, Guatemala, El Salvador, Honduras, Nicaragua, and Costa Rica formed a federation called the United Provinces of Central America (Belize was controlled by Great Britain and would not gain official independence until 1981; Panama was considered part of Colombia until gaining its independence in 1903). The federation was short-lived, however, and by 1827 the region was embroiled in internal conflicts. Civil war broke out in 1838, and the federation disintegrated.

cash crops: crops grown for sale rather than personal use.

During its short existence, the United Provinces of Central America did make one enduring accomplishment by establishing the boundaries of what became the nations of Central America.

Independence from Spain did not mean an end to the Native population's hardships either. Although no longer forced to pay tribute to the Spanish crown, a new type of enslavement began as plantations rose to grow *cash crops*. The elite classes now controlled much of Central America's land and used that land to grow crops like coffee, bananas, cotton, and sugarcane. For example, the coffee plant, which had been imported from Cuba in 1786, began being cultivated in Costa Rica in 1830. By 1845, that country was exporting coffee to England, and soon other Central American countries began growing the crop. By the 1880s, Central America was growing 14 percent of the world's coffee, and the coffee growers were the new ruling class of the area. The growth of coffee plantations in turn caused a shortage of labor, and forced labor became the rule. Eventually, class conflict would feed the fires of revolution as the poor majority itched to overthrow the wealthy minority.

In the unstable conditions caused by class inequality, *caudillos*, or dictators, rose up to govern the Central American nations. Some were relatively benign, but others were brutal and relied on military force to subdue their populations. Some, such as Rafael Carrera of Guatemala, also used their power to topple the governments of neighboring countries. For much of Central America, this internal strife would last throughout the twentieth century. Often these dictatorial governments lacked the support of the majority population, and numerous groups opposed their rule. Many dictatorships and oppressive governments, however, were difficult to overthrow because they had powerful friends at home and abroad.

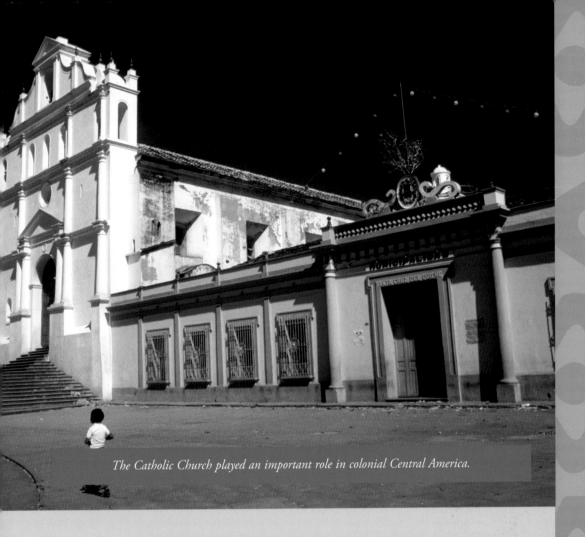

The Catholic Church played an important role in colonial Central America.

The Neighbor to the North

lthough the Spanish crown no longer governed Central American affairs, other foreign powers exerted important influence in the region. Another relatively young American nation, the United States, would prove to be the most important of these powers. The United States has long played an active role in Central America's power struggles by supporting certain governments, rulers, or organizations whose policies would benefit U.S. business and political interests.

The Panama Canal

An example of the United States' involvement in Central American affairs can be seen in the history of Panama. Plans for a canal across Central America had intrigued U.S. policy makers for years. Benjamin Franklin had even examined such plans before the American colonies declared their independence from Great Britain. By the mid-1800s, a gold rush was on in California, and everyone wanted an easier way to get from New York to San Francisco (a trip that, at the time, required a grueling overland journey). If only there were a way to make the trip by water without having to sail all the way around South America. The answer would be a canal dug through the narrowest section of the Central American isthmus. That section was in Panama.

The United States, however, couldn't just go to a foreign country and embark on the largest man-made construction project in the world. At the time, Colombia controlled Panama, and no agreements for the canal could be reached. But not everyone in Panama wanted to remain part of Colombia, and factions were fighting for independence. The United States was willing to strike a deal: it would provide military support for Panama's independence if Panama gave the United States permission to build and control the canal. In 1902, the United States landed troops in Panama, and in 1903 Panama declared its independence. The United States quickly recognized the new country, and work on the canal began almost immediately.

The United States also actively intervened in Nicaragua when U.S. President William Taft sent troops to support a *puppet government* there. U.S. forces took control of the national bank, railroad, and customs office, and in 1916 the country was formally recognized as a U.S. *protectorate*. Despite opposition from the Nicaraguans, the U.S. Marines remained in Nicaragua until 1933. Cesar Augusto Sandino, a former army officer, led a seven-year *guerrilla* struggle against the occupation. In 1934, Sandino was murdered during a supposed truce and became a *martyr* for Nicaraguan independence.

puppet government: a government whose actions are controlled by others.

protectorate: a country or region that is defended and controlled by a more powerful state.

guerrilla: irregular military unit committing harsh warfare and sabotage.

martyr: someone who chooses to die rather than deny religious or political beliefs.

Economic Dependence

ot everyone agreed that it was appropriate for the United States to use military intervention in Central American affairs. Under Presidents Herbert Hoover and repercussions: things, often unexpected, that result from an action.

"The definite policy of the United States from now on is one opposed to armed intervention."
—President Franklin D. Roosevelt

Franklin D. Roosevelt, the United States adopted the "Good Neighbor" policy toward Latin America. President Roosevelt declared: "In the field of world policy I would dedicate this nation to the policy of the good neighbor—the neighbor who resolutely respects himself and, because he does so, respects the rights of others." Throughout the 1930s, the stated goal was to cease military involvement in the region in favor of diplomatic and economic interventions.

One of the things the Good Neighbor policy did was give Central American exports special access to U.S. markets. While this change in policy was welcome, it could not guarantee improvement in the Central American economies. When the Great Depression hit in the 1930s, Central America soon felt the *repercussions*. Coffee and banana exports declined sharply. The economic turmoil spurred popular uprisings, the largest of which occurred in El Salvador where as many as 30,000 peasants were killed when the army suppressed a revolt. Even once the initial crisis had passed, unemployment rates remained stubbornly high and wages stagnated.

More of the Same?

Presidents Hoover and Roosevelt may have tried to change the United States' policies toward Central America, but throughout the second half of the twentieth century U.S. administrations found many ways, military and otherwise, to support certain people and governments. The United States, however, did not just play a role in keeping certain people in power.

Theodore Roosevelt

deposed: removed from office.

agrarian: an economy based on agriculture.

Cold War: the period of hostile, nonviolent relations between the Soviet Union, the United States, and their allies from 1946 to 1989.

coup: the sudden overthrow of a government.

covert: secret, not intended to be known.

overt: open, obvious.

It also played an important role in keeping other people out of power. For example, in 1944, Guatemala's dictator was *deposed*, and soon dramatic changes occurred. The people of Guatemala elected President Juan Jose Arevalo in that country's first free and fair elections. Arevalo was a former philosophy professor who believed in land reform and workers' rights, which made him hugely unpopular with the country's wealthy elite. In 1949, his minister of defense, Jacobo Arbenz, succeeded Arevalo as President and proposed even more *agrarian* reforms.

Arbenz faced concerted opposition from the United Fruit Company, a U.S. business that had long benefited from the dictatorship in Guatemala but stood to lose from Arevalo's and Arbenz's pro-labor policies. The company persuaded the U.S. government that Arbenz was a communist sympathizer. In these early days of the *Cold War*, the charge was deadly. U.S.-trained forces invaded the country, and in 1954 a military *coup* forced Arbenz to resign.

The U.S. involvement in the region grew throughout the 1960s, with *covert* and *overt* support for right-wing dictators. The region's economy also continued to be dominated by the export of products such as coffee and bananas. Throughout the region, a small minority of people continued to hold the vast majority of wealth, while most of the population struggled with grinding poverty. The income disparities fueled revolutionary sentiments, especially as the middle class saw that U.S.-backed development plans failed to increase income levels substantially. Rapid population growth led to increased food and land shortages. Unemployment levels were dangerously high. In El Salvador in 1965, for example, 40 percent of the population was underemployed or unemployed.

Conditions had long been ripe for economic and social change, but the fight was difficult and bitter throughout the re-

Poverty is an ongoing problem in Central America.

Guatemala countryside

gion. In Nicaragua, the *Frente de Liberacion Nacional*, popularly known as Sandinistas after the martyred independence leader Sandino, began fighting the Anastasio Somoza dictatorship in 1961 and took power in 1979. President Ronald Reagan's administration responded by funding an armed rebellion against the Sandinista government, contrary to the express desire of the U.S. Congress.

Ronald Reagan

The Reagan administration also gave vital support to the military government in El Salvador, where a right-wing dictatorship brutally suppressed its opponents with death squads, killing 1,000 people every month by 1981. Only after Reagan left office did peace negotiations succeed in El Salvador, and in 1992 the rebel groups and the government signed a peace treaty. Following the peace accord in El Salvador, a U.N. commission determined that the government and its death-squad allies had committed about 85 percent of the human rights violations during the civil war.

Guatemala also suffered through a decades-long civil war as a brutal political dictatorship refused to consider democratic reforms. Under the administration of General Romeo Lucas Garcia thousands of Guatemalans—Maya, labor leaders, students, and intellectuals—were murdered. General Efrain Rios Montt seized power in 1982, pledging army reforms, but the killing continued. Human rights groups in 1982 estimated that the army and its paramilitary allies had killed 9,000 Guatemalans in the five previous months. The United States sent $15.5 million to support the Guatemalan government that year.

The conflicts in El Salvador and Guatemala were both resolved as part of a regional peace plan advocated by

The military plays an ongoing role in Central America.

President Arias of Costa Rica. The preliminary peace plan was drafted in 1987. It called for *democratization*, *amnesties*, and cease-fires in Guatemala, Nicaragua, and El Salvador. The United Nations assisted the negotiations, which finally stopped the conflicts in Nicaragua in 1990, in El Salvador in 1992, and in Guatemala in 1996. By the time these cease-fires had been established, about 300,000 Central Americans had been killed, and about two million Central Americans had become refugees.

democratization: the process of giving control of a country to its citizens through free and equal decision-making powers.

amnesties: pardons.

hese events created turmoil in Central America that eventually forced people to flee their homes. In the United States, the refugees faced the challenge of building new lives. Meanwhile, ongoing conditions would continue to drive more Central Americans north.

Habla Español

campesinos (com-pay-see-noes): country people

paz (pahs): peace

Estados Unidos (ace-tah-dose oo-nee-dose): United States

3

Refugees from Unrest

Supaya Serrano can still see her sisters, ages three and seven, by the hill where they met the soldiers.

"I was hearing all that shooting and I was scared, so I told the kids, 'Please stay here, I'm going to get away a little further, so that they don't find us all together,'" Serrano remembers.

That was May of 1982. When she returned to the spot later that day, the two girls were gone. They have never been found. Many people suspect that the Salvadoran Army took Serrano's sisters, along with other children, and sold them for profit.

47

A peaceful Central American street does not reveal the area's ongoing political conflict.

atricia Valle lived in the Morazan province of El Salvador in the early 1980s. When her partner was accused of being a guerrilla fighter, he fled to Mexico. Valle, however, remained behind. Members of the death squads who terrorized the countryside came to her house, seeking information from her. They tortured and raped her in front of her children. Miraculously, she survived and fled first to Guatemala and then to Mexico. After an earthquake struck Mexico City in 1985, destroying their possessions, Valle and her family moved to the United States. She was one of more than one million Salvadorans who fled during the civil war in their country.

Children often suffer the most during times of war and upheaval.

asylum: a place of safety and protection.

Isaac Paiz knew the signs—the anonymous phone calls, the rumors—and he knew what these signs meant. Many people who did not heed them were killed by the death squads that helped the Guatemalan government stay in power.

Paiz, a university student in Guatemala City, was in danger because he opposed the government. He decided to pay attention to the hints that he might be the next death-squad victim. He fled, first to Mexico and then to the United States.

That was in 1992. Paiz has done a lot of running and a lot of hiding since then. He arrived in California about ten years ago, but he was not a legal immigrant. As a consequence, he had to accept the jobs that many Americans disdain and work for lower pay than minimum-wage laws require. For ten years, he worked mainly in restaurants and the construction industry. "It's hard, because you can't get ahead when you are just working in restaurants or digging ditches. You're a slave in America, working for $3 an hour for nine or ten hours a day," Paiz said. He spent eight years in legal limbo before his claim for political *asylum* was accepted.

Since he achieved legal status, however, Paiz's economic condition has improved substantially. Now the father of two girls born in the United States, Paiz runs a small store in Miami Beach that sells jewelry and clothing.

persecution: the subjecting of a group of people to cruel or unfair treatment.

Supaya Serrano's, Patricia Valle's, and Isaac Paiz's stories are far from unusual. Immigrants from Central America form the fastest-growing portion of the Latino community in the United States. Knowing the history of repression in the countries of Central America, it isn't hard to understand their motivation for leaving. The brutality of governments—some, like that in El Salvador, actively supported by the United States—forced people to flee for their lives. Serrano, Valle, and Paiz were lucky. They made it to the United States. Many were not so lucky. Furthermore, once arriving, many Central Americans found that the United States was not the refuge they believed it would be.

Denied Status

Throughout the 1980s and 1990s, Central American refugees fleeing persecution poured into the United States. In 1980, the U.S. government had passed the Refugee Act to ensure refugees would be admitted and resettled in the country. Refugees were defined as individuals who were unable or unwilling to return to their homeland because of *persecution* or a well-founded fear of persecution. People like Supaya Serrano, Patricia Valle, Isaac Paiz, and many other Central Americans fled their homes precisely because they feared for their safety, even for their lives. Nevertheless, it has been virtually impossible for most Central Americans to receive refugee status and get the protection and benefits due refugees under the law.

Central American families sought refuge in the United States.

Immigrants unite in protest.

One of the biggest reasons it was so difficult for most Central Americans to receive refugee status was that it was the official position of the U.S. government that countries such as El Salvador did not commit human rights abuses. The streams of refugees clearly indicated that El Salvador did, indeed, have a serious human rights problem. The U.S. government, nonetheless, was committed to supporting the government of El Salvador, so much so that by the early 1980s, the country became the third-largest recipient of U.S. aid worldwide.

Economic assistance given by the U.S. government to the rulers of El Salvador was *contingent* on the Salvadoran government guaranteeing that it was making progress in controlling human rights abuses. But not only did the human rights violations not subside, the billions of dollars in aid did little to improve the quality of life for the poor. The unemployment rate was about 40 percent by 1983, and most Salvadorans could barely feed their families. Clearly, a mix of economic and political reasons motivated people fleeing El Salvador and other turbulent countries in the area, but the Reagan administration and the subsequent Bush administration denied asylum to hundreds of thousands of

Elderly Central American women and a grandchild wait for a bus.

Salvadorans and other Central American refugees. The U.S. government believed these people were fleeing poverty rather than fleeing direct persecution, so it termed many of these people "economic refugees" and accorded them no special status.

Whatever their motivations, many people were fleeing El Salvador in the early 1980s. Between 1980 and 1982, the illegal Salvadoran population in the United States grew from about 94,000 to between 300,000 and 500,000. Similarly, Guatemalans were fleeing into Mexico at a rate of 2,000 to 3,500 per week. Asylum, however, was rarely granted to these displaced people. Only .9 percent of Guatemalan and 2.6 percent of Salvadoran appeals for asylum were granted between June 1983 and September 1986. Refugees from governments deemed unfriendly to the United States stood a much better chance of being granted asylum. For example, more than 60

contingent: dependent.

atrocities: extremely
evil or cruel acts, often
during war.

sanctuary: a place of
safety or refuge.

percent of Iranians seeking asylum during the same period had their petitions approved.

The threats from the death squads abated for the most part throughout Central America following the peace accords signed in the 1990s. Many of those who committed *atrocities* in the previous two decades, however, remain in powerful positions and prosecutions of human rights abuse cases have been few. Those people who pursue such cases do so at their peril.

Finding Sanctuary

Despite the U.S. government's refusal to acknowledge Central Americans' refugee status, many private citizens recognized that the people fleeing Central America were in grave danger and needed help.

The plight of the Central American refugees, specifically those from violence-shrouded El Salvador and Guatemala, first came to national attention in July 1980 when twenty-seven Salvadorans were discovered in Arizona's Organ Pipe Cactus National Monument. Their coyote (a person who smuggles people over the southern U.S. border) had abandoned them, and thirteen of them had already died of dehydration. As their stories were told, the full scale of government oppression in El Salvador became public as never before. When the surviving Salvadorans were arrested and threatened with deportation, outraged community members posted bail and gave the refugees *sanctuary* in local churches.

Over the objections of the U.S. government, other churches

Miami is now home to many wealthy Salvadorans.

A Sad Irony

Ironically, while the U.S. government denied refugee status to thousands, it allowed between 150 and 300 families from El Salvador's wealthy ruling class to settle in Miami. A U.N. Truth Commission later found that many of these immigrants were able to establish a base outside of their country to direct the death squads that terrorized the countryside of El Salvador.

Churches played prominent roles in the Sanctuary Movement.

and organizations began assisting refugees in what came to be known as the Sanctuary Movement. On January 14, 1985, however, the U.S. Immigration and Naturalization Service arrested refugees given sanctuary by congregations of the American Baptists in Seattle; Washington; and Rochester, New York. On the same day, sixteen people associated with the Sanctuary Movement were *indicted* in Phoenix, Arizona. Despite government pressure, the movement continued. According to Martha Liebler Gibson of the University of Colorado–Boulder, the Sanctuary Movement eventually grew to include more than 400 churches and 2,000 other sympathetic organizations.

New Threats in a New Age

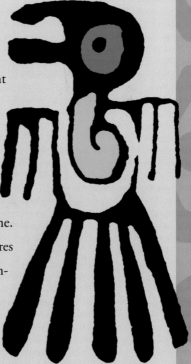

indicted: *formally charged with a crime.*

oday, Central America's death squads and government persecution are largely things of the past, but people living in Central America continue to face threats to their security and health. For the most part, the Arias Peace Accords ended the bitter political violence that raged across the region for two decades, but the social causes that led to the violence still pose a threat to the long-term social and political stability of the region. Central American countries in general are characterized by extremes of wealth and poverty, and the roots of democracy in the region do not extend deeply.

The greatest threats to democracy and stability in Central America today come not from dictators and brutal military governments but from economic conditions. Central America is afflicted with high debt levels and stagnant economies, the results many say of misguided economic policies dictated by the United States. Just look at the percentage of the population deemed poor from data gathered in 2002. In Costa Rica, traditionally the most democratic, stable, and prosperous Central American country, about 9.5 percent of the population lived below the poverty line. That's approximately one out of ten people. And the figures were substantially higher for the other Central American countries. Panama's poverty rate was 17.6 percent, meaning nearly one out of five people lived in poverty. Guatemala's rate was 37.4 percent, more than one out of three people. Honduras had the next largest poverty rate at 44.4 percent. In El Salvador, well over half the population, 58 percent, was

Becoming Legal

Immigration law, naturally, is one of the critical areas of concern for Central Americans who have settled in the United States. The issue of immigration has been a contentious political concern for more than a century, and immigration laws are changed regularly to adjust to political, social, or economic realities. In 1990, for example, a 1986 law designed to target employers hiring undocumented workers was used to deny work to refugees. After the September 11, 2001, attacks on the United States, laws on immigration became more stringent and more tightly enforced. By 2004, the Department of Homeland Security had issued rules that allowed streamlined deportation procedures for Central Americans.

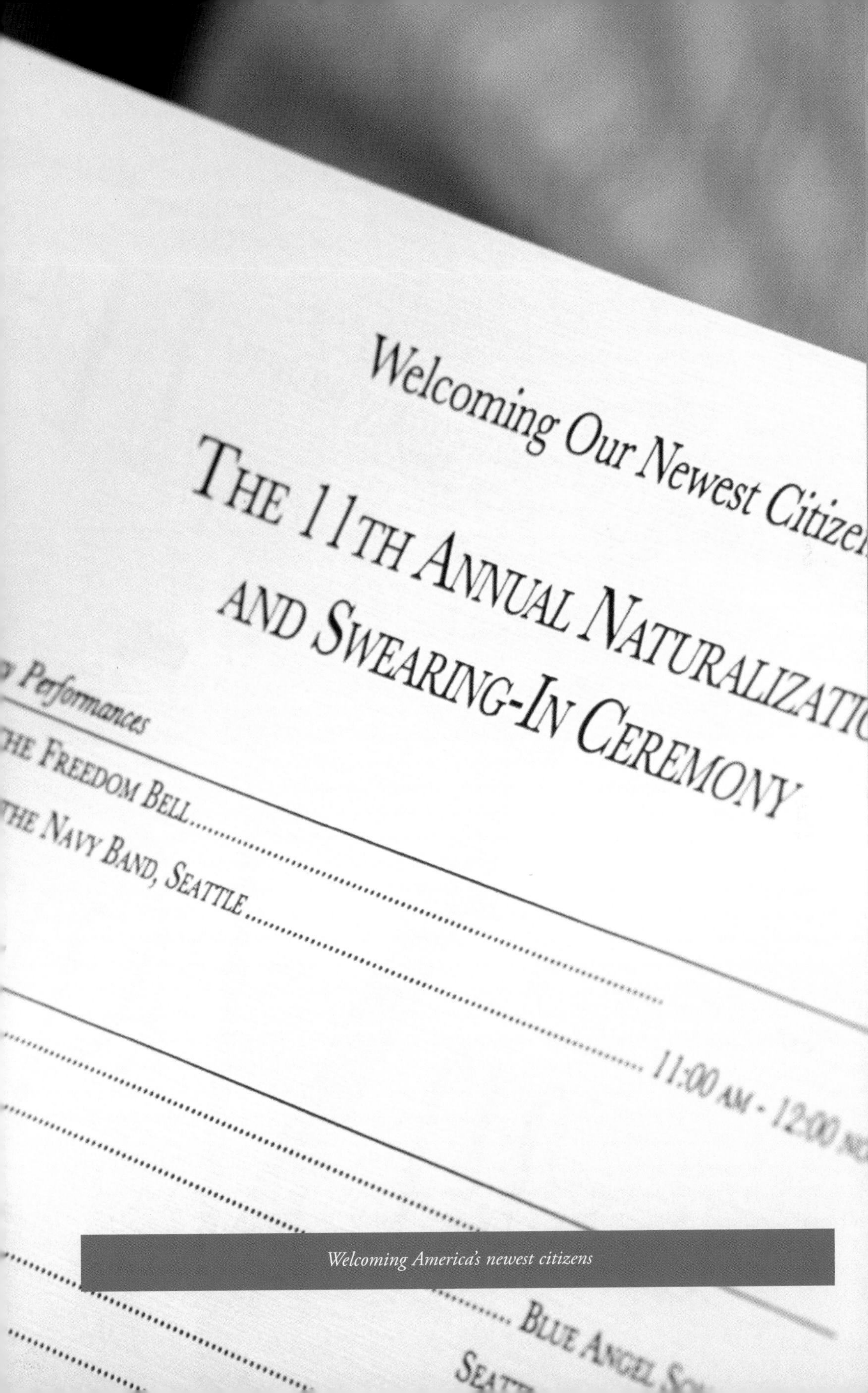

Welcoming Our Newest Citizen

THE 11TH ANNUAL NATURALIZATIO
AND SWEARING-IN CEREMONY

Performances

THE FREEDOM BELL..

THE NAVY BAND, SEATTLE..

.... 11:00 AM - 12:00 N

Welcoming America's newest citizens

.... BLUE ANGEL SC

SEATTL

Most of these Central Americans live in poverty.

living in poverty; and in Nicaragua, a shocking 79.9 percent of the population, more than two out of every three people, lived in poverty.

Of course, with poor economic conditions come the problems they foster—most notably crime. Central Americans may no longer fear government-sponsored death squads, but high crime rates mean many people's lives are still in danger. Violent crime cost the lives of more than 10,000 Central Americans in 2002. The violent crime rate is almost twenty-eight incidents per 100,000 residents, roughly five times the rate in the United States. *Maras*, or street gangs, are widespread and responsible for a large amount of the region's crime. The extent of the mara problem varies widely among the Central American republics. In Nicaragua, police officials estimate there are only sixty-two gangs with about 1,000 members. Guatemala, however, has about 14,000 gang members, El Salvador has 10,500, and Honduras has 36,000. The gangs are difficult to conquer, because when law enforcement tightens in one area, the gangs simply move to another area (or even to a neighboring country) where law enforcement is less effective. As a result, leaders in Central America are seeking a coordinated response to the problem so that a crackdown in one country doesn't just push the problem elsewhere. In 2003, El Salvador launched a new program called "*Mano Super Dura*" to clamp down on teenage street gangs. Panama and Honduras launched their own similar programs the following year.

Overall, the governments blame the maras for much of the region's crime, but crimes don't just happen on the street. Central America also wrestles with government corruption, which saps vital funds and breeds *cynicism* among the populace. In Guatemala, for example, the President promised to purge completely the national police after discovering that the police themselves were members of a gang accused of murder and extortion. A former Vice President of Guatemala was also arrested in 2004 and charged with stealing $2.4 million in government property.

Poverty and crime are perhaps the most visible threats to Central America's stability, but there are also other less obvious threats against the region's people. One of the most serious growing threats is AIDS (acquired immunodeficiency syndrome). Honduras currently has the highest level of AIDS among the Central American nations, with about 60 percent of the AIDS cases in the region. In addition to those with AIDS, the government estimates that about 65,000 Hondurans have contracted the HIV virus that causes the disease. AIDS now is second only to street violence as a cause of death.

High HIV and AIDS rates spell future disaster not only for those living with the disease but also for the entire region. The majority of the people living with and dying from AIDS are

cynicism: an expression of a distrusting attitude.

Immigrants demand America's attention to the ongoing violence in Latin America.

young adults—the portion of the population raising the most children and working at the most jobs. AIDS, therefore, is killing Central America's parents and workers. Who will care for the children, sick, and elderly, and who will support these countries' economies if a huge portion of the young-adult population dies? According to a U.N. study, at least 25,500 children have been orphaned in Honduras alone because their parents died of AIDS. Now these children have no parents to guide them as they grow, and the huge cost of caring for these parentless children falls to the debt-strained government.

hether it was the violence of the past or the economic instability, crime, and other desperate conditions of the present, there have been and continue to be many reasons for Central Americans to seek a better life in the United States. But getting to the United States and surviving once there is much more difficult than many people would imagine. Not only can the journey into the United States be long and dangerous, but many challenges await those who successfully complete the journey.

Habla Español

gobierna (go-bee-air-nah): government

niños (neen-yoes): children

guerra (gare-rah): war

riqueza (ree-kay-sah): riches, wealth

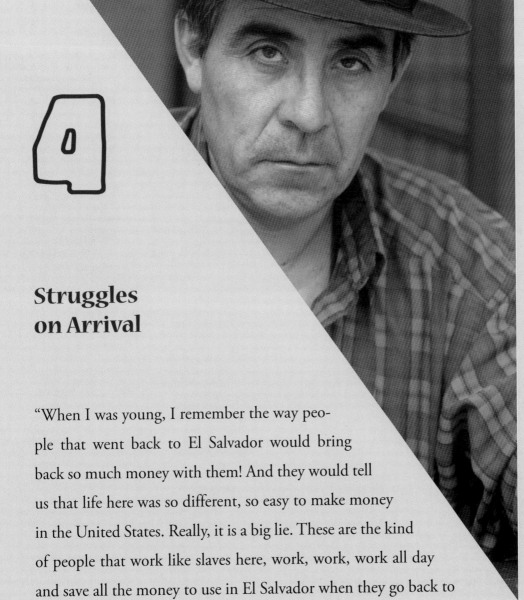

Struggles on Arrival

"When I was young, I remember the way people that went back to El Salvador would bring back so much money with them! And they would tell us that life here was so different, so easy to make money in the United States. Really, it is a big lie. These are the kind of people that work like slaves here, work, work, work all day and save all the money to use in El Salvador when they go back to show it off back there. They don't use any of their money here. So when I came in, I encountered all these other problems here too."

—Raul, seventeen-year-old refugee from El Salvador

Many Central American immigrants are seeking to escape the poverty of their homelands.

The Road to the United States

an you imagine what it would be like to leave your home, family, friends, job, and everything you have ever known? Now imagine moving someplace where everything from the culture to the language to the climate was different. Whether you are a refugee or an immigrant, moving to a new country is a difficult, emotional decision that most people don't take lightly. It's frightening and sad to leave your home, and you wouldn't choose to do so unless motivated by very strong forces. Nevertheless, many immigrants arrive in the United States with a great deal of hope. But what do they find once they arrive? Does the United States prove to be the land of opportunity they dreamed of? For many immigrants, traveling to the United States and adjusting once they have arrived present harsh realities. Some Central Americans find that the events of their past make it particularly difficult to adjust to life in a new land.

Different People, Different Paths

ach immigrant to the United States has his or her own story, and there are more than a couple of paths to becoming an immigrant—legal or illegal—in the United States. Many Central American immigrants make their way to the United States in a dangerous overland migration along well-trod trails through Mexico and into the American Southwest. This path of immigration is made more difficult by the "*Plan Sur*" that Mexico started in 2001, which uses Mexico's southern border as a buffer specifically against illegal immigration from Central America.

Just crossing Mexico is dangerous for immigrants. Many are attacked by criminals; at least seventy immigrants were killed in Mexico by gangs in 2003. The immigrants cannot expect much better treatment by Mexican authorities. If they are caught, they may be held indefinitely in overcrowded and unsanitary detention facilities. Despite the difficulties, the flow of immigrants through Mexico continues to increase. In 2003, Mexico deported 147,000 illegal immigrants, an increase of about 20 percent over the previous year. Most of the immigrants came from Guatemala, Nicaragua, and Honduras.

Mexico's desert can be dangerous to cross.

Even if they are not caught in Mexico, the trip is dangerous, requiring a desert crossing. Dozens of immigrants die every year in the desert area of Arizona alone. The problem has prompted volunteers to assist the immigrants. A group called Human Borders, for example, has set up water tanks in the desert for those trying to make the difficult crossing. Other groups are setting up civilian patrols that search the desert for stranded immigrants, obtaining emergency medical care for them. But not all the people immigrants encounter in the desert mean to be helpful. Recently, growing numbers of armed citizens' militias (vigilante groups operating with no authority from law enforcement or the government) have taken to patrolling areas of the southern border to keep out immigrants.

Even if they make it through the desert, immigrants face tightened border security and tougher new regulations. In the summer of 2004, the Department of Homeland Security announced rules that give border officers broad authority to bypass

immigration courts, quickly deporting illegal immigrants other than Mexicans and Canadians. Many Central Americans try to pretend that they are Mexicans because the treatment by the Border Patrol may be more lenient.

Not all immigrants, however, trek across the desert to reach the United States. Rhina Garcia, for example, was working as a nurse in Guatemala City when a woman approached her and offered her a job in the United States. The woman, a relative of a diplomat working in Washington, had been sent by the diplomat's family to find a responsible woman to work as a live-in nanny. Garcia, who had dreamed of living in the United States, took the job. Already

The U.S.-Mexican border is more closely patrolled since September 11, 2001.

guaranteed legal employment saved Garcia from braving the illegal crossing; she could simply take a flight to her new home.

Once in the United States, Garcia discovered (as many immigrants do) that her new job didn't pay much for the amount of labor involved. She quit that job and the next one she found before she landed a position that suited her. Ten years later, she was married and had acquired permanent residency. As happens with many immigrants, Garcia's success rippled through her family connections. Over the last decade, two brothers, two sisters, her parents, several cousins, and many friends joined her in the Washington, D.C., area. They, in turn, assisted other Guatemalans.

Supporting Families Back Home

Perhaps because of its diplomatic community and a large market for household help, the Washington, D.C., area has become a key settlement area for immigrants from Central America. About half of the immigrants from Central America said they came to Washington because they already had a relative living in the area. Many also say that they've heard there are more jobs and better pay in Washington, D.C. Some towns in Central America have even become comparatively wealthy because of the money sent from people's relatives living and working in the United States. The town of Intipuca, El Salvador, renamed one of its major roads Washington Street in honor of the financial support sent home from there.

Census: when capitalized, the constitutionally required counting of the U.S. population every ten years.

Counting a Shadow Population

How many Central Americans there are in the United States is hard to determine exactly. In 1980, the federal *Census* counted 331,219 people who had been born in Central

Central American students

Central American immigrants are a growing segment of the U.S. population.

America. During the Central American turmoil of the 1980s, however, that number increased dramatically. In 1990, 1,323,830 people of Central American descent were counted. Ten years later, the figure was 1,685,937, representing more than a 27 percent increase. Of these Central Americans immigrants, El Salvadorans were the most numerous, representing 655,000 of the total. They were followed by Guatemalans (372,000), Hondurans (218,000), and Nicaraguans (178,000). Panamanians and Costa Ricans represented 92,000 and 69,000, respectively.

Today, El Salvador continues to contribute the most Central American immigrants to the United States for a variety of reasons. Its population density, meaning the number of people who live within a given area, historically has been higher than that of other Central

American countries. That means that Salvadorans tend to live in more crowded conditions and have greater competition for resources than people living elsewhere in the region. El Salvador has also experienced rapid population growth. By the end of the 1980s, almost half of its population was under the age of fifteen, figures that promised population growth would only rise as these young people got older and began having children of their own. To make matters worse, roughly half of El Salvador lives below the poverty line, and the country still suffers from enormous disparities in income. The situation may have improved some since 1985, when roughly one percent of the population controlled 40 percent of farmland, but not much. The CIA estimated in 2004 that in El Salvador, the richest 10 percent of the population represents about 40 percent of the nation's spending.

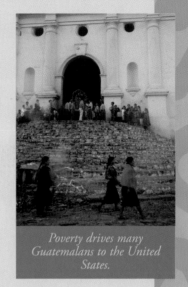

Poverty drives many Guatemalans to the United States.

Guatemala, the largest of the Central American countries, also contributes many immigrants to the United States. Before a peace agreement was signed in 1996, more than one million refugees had fled the country to escape its civil war, which was the longest-running civil war of any country in Latin America. Now poverty is a prime motivation for Guatemalans leaving their country. More than 65 percent of the country's population lives in extreme poverty. In June 2004, the nation was paralyzed by a nationwide strike as a coalition of diverse groups protested the evictions of indigenous people from their farms. The President of the country pledged to stop the violent evictions and take steps to assist farmers, but many doubted his commitment. In Guatemala, more than 80 percent of the 5.5 million small farmers fall below the poverty line, so major changes will be necessary if their lot is to be improved. In addition to providing many immigrants to the United States, Guatemala also acts as a transit area for people from other

Central American countries who eventually immigrate to the United States.

Nicaraguan immigrants to the United States have been of several varieties. There were Nicaraguans who fled the brutal Somoza dictatorship that was overthrown in 1979. Then there were Nicaraguans who fled the socialist Sandinista regime that ousted Somoza. Perhaps the largest group, however, was simply fleeing the overall violence in the country as the Sandinista government fought off the U.S.-funded Contra forces. Between 1966 and 1977, Nicaragua contributed the fewest legally admitted immigrants to the United States of any country in Central America, but by the end of the 1970s, the level was similar to that of other countries. By 1986, more than half a million Nicaraguans had been displaced from their homeland.

For many years, Honduras experienced more stability than other Central American countries and thus contributed few immigrants to the United States. In fact, Honduras actually accepted many refugees from other Central American countries, with these immigrants representing almost three percent of the population in 1986. In recent years, however, immigration from Honduras to the United States has been increasing but more gradually than that of other countries.

Once inside the United States, immigrants often settle together to form communities. This way, they live among people with similar cultures and experiences to their own and find support among their neighbors. Therefore, certain areas of the United States have much larger Central American populations than other areas. For example, Salvadorans are now the largest Latino group in Washington, D.C. Los Angeles also has a large Salvadoran population, with almost two-fifths of the Salvadoran population in the United States living in that region. Guatemalans are also attracted to Los Angeles, with almost 50 percent of them living in that metropolitan area.

Many Central Americans have settled in Los Angeles.

Nicaraguans and Hondurans, however, are settling in the Gulf Coast region, with many putting down roots in southern Florida and New Orleans.

Bearing Scars

aking it to the United States, however, does not mean a person's problems are over. Central American immigrants to the United States face an assortment of challenges in this country. Some of these challenges are common to all newcomers, but others are specific to those coming from Central America. The brutality that many Central Americans endured before arriving in the United States presents its own difficulty. Thousands bear the psychological, spiritual, and physical scars inflicted during years of violence.

Central Americans often provide support for one another.

Over the years, immigrants from Central America simply referred to "*La situacion*" as their motivation for leaving their homelands. This can refer to everything from murder, rape, and torture to forced recruitment into armed forces. While the immediate threats of violence no longer may be the main motivation for coming to the United States, "La situacion" caused real physical and emotional damage that continues to affect many Central American immigrants today. One California study in 2000, for example, found that 72 percent of Central American immigrants reported suffering trauma such as physical or sexual assault. This was the highest rate of any immigrant group studied. Another psychological study of Central American immigrants found that when contemplating a drawing of an adolescent boy and doctor, 45 percent of the respondents believed the drawing depicted a scene of torture or assassination. Most Korean immigrants, by comparison, thought that the picture showed a hero in a medical operation.

La Clinica del Pueblo in Washington, D.C., pays close attention to the stresses that may be affecting their Central American patients. The clinic was formed in 1983 by a coalition of U.S. and Central American residents concerned about the health care offered to Latinos. A bicultural and bilingual clinic, it offers free care to Latinos, over 70 percent of whom are from Central America. The clinic's cultural-sensitivity manual lists the following as causes of stress common to Central American immigrants: previous trauma, unresolved legal status, fear of deportation, lack of financial security, unemployment, overcrowded housing, and divided families.

Just the process of immigrating to the United States is stressful for many Central American families. According to one mental health survey of Central Americans, about one-half of those surveyed showed signs of depression. Depression was often associated with separation from family, and even legal immigrants were affected. Increased stress levels led to other problems like increased drinking of alcohol.

Another study of Central Americans and other immigrants found that 85 percent of immigrant children become separated from one or both parents during the move to the United States. These children may get separated from their parents when authorities stop their family members. Many times these children end up traveling the rest of the way to the United States with close relatives or friends. When they arrive in the United States, they frequently find shelter with extended family or friends of the family. The situation of Central American children was worse than other groups studied; 80 percent of them had become separated from both parents. Nearly half of the Central Americans had been apart from their mothers for more than five years.

Education is an important aspect of adapting to U.S. culture.

This study also found that the children who had been separated from their parents experienced higher rates of depression. Many times, the children didn't remember their parents when they were reintroduced. Naturally, the children were less likely to give their parents respect. Educators also said that the lack of authority figures for children affects their success in school.

Educational Challenges

Education is a particularly important issue for Central Americans. Education is essential for immigrants hoping to succeed in the United States, yet many Central Americans begin their life in the United States with an educational disadvantage.

Roughly 27 percent of the patients served at the Washington, D.C., free clinic cannot read or write. Many of them come from rural communities where access to education was limited. The wars in the region destroyed educational facilities and killed many teachers. Economic conditions also forced children to drop out of school in order to work to help support their families. The people who do finish primary school are deemed highly educated by their communities, although they may be considered illiterate in the United States. One study in California found that more than 70 percent of the Central American immigrants lacked a high school diploma, compared to 26 percent for Southeast Asians and 14 percent for East Asians.

Academic excellence for its own sake, however, is not necessarily a goal for many Central Americans coming to the United States. Marcelo Suarez-Orozco, who studied Central American

"My mother has been here ten years, without even a high school diploma. She went only to the second grade of high school in Guatemala. Then she had to work. When she came here it was so hard for her. She was all alone with no family here. She spoke no English. I now want to help her, so she does not have to continue to work anymore. That is the only thing I have to do. This is why I am undecided about going to the university or going to work. She wants me to do what I desire, but. . . . Well, for me it would not be correct not to work because of the way she has helped us."

—Jose, seventeen-year-old Guatemalan immigrant

refugees in U.S. high schools, found that the Central American students were motivated by less individualistic concerns than their Anglo cohorts. The young people Suarez-Orozco studied had "a wish to achieve in order to nurture one's parents and other less-fortunate relatives. This specific familistic charity, surely related to a broader concept of religious charity that has flourished through the Central American religious landscape in the past three decades, was rediscovered and intensified as the immigrants settled in the new land."

Clearly, education is critically important for Central Americans, or any immigrant group, to move ahead in the United States. Unfortunately, higher education is closed to many Central American youths because of their illegal status. Mirtha Colon, director of the Organization of Black Central Americans, said her organization is working with others to help open the doors to college for Central American immigrants.

A Central American mother and daughter

While public primary and secondary schools are open to illegal immigrant children, Colon said legal barriers still exist for Central Americans who wish to continue their studies at colleges and universities in the United States. Without the possibility of higher education, she said, Central American students will have lower motivation to excel in high school and will be trapped in a cycle of low expectations.

Earning Their Way

In the United States, Central American immigrants have gained a reputation for their strong work ethic. Nevertheless, Central American immigrants often find themselves stuck in poorly paid, low-status jobs by U.S. standards. One problem is that if an immigrant comes to the United States without proper authorization, he will be forced to work illegally. Plenty of American employers are happy to hire illegal workers because they can pay these workers lower wages than they pay legal workers. Furthermore, employers of illegal workers escape giving the costly benefits (like health care) and paying the taxes associated with legal employees. This situation saves the employer money, but it traps the illegal immigrant into low-wage, benefit-less, and even dangerous employment. Furthermore, since he is illegally employed in the first place, the immigrant has no legal protection if, for instance, he should get hurt on the job or be treated unfairly.

Another problem immigrants face is that their employment qualifications often go unrecognized. The education, licenses, and certifications they may have received in Central America rarely transfer to the United States. For instance, if an immigrant was a lawyer in Central America, she cannot be a lawyer in the United States without completing her entire education over again and receiving all new U.S. qualifications (something few immigrants can afford to do). Many highly educated Central Americans end up working dead-end, low-wage jobs in the "land of opportunity."

Unlike immigrants from some other regions, Central Americans frequently leave their countries as fractured families. In one survey of Central American women in the Washington, D.C., area, two-thirds declared that they didn't come to the United States with a male partner; the decision to come was theirs. Sometimes they were fleeing violence at home, and sometimes they were simply looking for a better life. Perhaps as a consequence of the situations in their countries, Central American women have displayed an unusual level of autonomy. The women who did come alone, however, did have high to moderate levels of education and came directly from the capital cities in their countries.

Central American women can face particular hardships because they are often *stereotyped* for employment. Many employers believe that Central American women will be especially warm and nurturing for children, so Central American women are frequently sought for domestic help. Like Rhina Garcia (who we spoke of earlier in this chapter), who was a nurse before coming to the United States, many of these women have a good deal of education and additional skills. Nevertheless, they find themselves employed as domestic servants with few prospects for moving up to other careers.

Central American women in general have higher levels of education than their male counterparts, but they earn less than most male immigrants. Whereas Central American women are often employed in domestic service, many Central American men find their employment in the construction business. In one survey, 53 percent of Central American men were working in the construction business. These jobs generally pay better than other jobs, like those in the restaurant business—another common employer of Central American immigrants. According to the same survey, roughly one-quarter of Central American men worked in the restaurant business, with the construction workers earning roughly three dollars more an hour than the restaurant workers. Another quarter of those surveyed worked in assorted businesses such as pool cleaning and factory work.

stereotyped: judged based on incomplete and often inaccurate information.

A Few Outside the Law

Despite the difficulties immigrants face on arrival in the United States, the vast majority do find employment and become productive, contributing members of society. However, a certain number of immigrants (like a certain number of American-born citizens) turn to illegal activities to support themselves. Perhaps they do this because they are having

methamphetamines:
stimulant drugs.

Gang violence is a characteristic of a small minority of Central American immigrants.

difficulty finding a good-paying job, or perhaps they were involved in criminal activities before coming to the United States. Whatever the reasons, in recent years gangs linked to Central American cities have developed in the United States. For example, Mara Salvatrucha, which has ties to El Salvador, has become established in the Washington, D.C., area. And gangs are not just an urban problem. In one rural area of Georgia, ten Latino gangs have marked out their territories.

The gangs run enterprises such as dealing in *methamphetamines* and prey on isolated immigrant communities. Many of the gangs have been pushed out of the metropolitan areas and take advantage of the poorly funded law enforcement in the rural areas.

Some of the new Latino gangs are influenced by the climate of violence that for so long dominated Central America. Often separated from their parents and traumatized by violence, many of the new gang members include veterans from both sides in the civil wars. They have been exposed to horrific violence and trained in the use of weapons. Not surprisingly, their attitude toward violence is casual. The new gangs from Central America, particularly Mara Salvatrucha, have become notorious for their brutality. In 2004, Mara Salvatrucha had about 1,500 gang members in northern Virginia and was blamed for at least six murders in the state.

Gangs like Mara Salvatrucha make life even more difficult for Central American immigrants. Not only do the gangs prey on the poor immigrant communities, but they have bad reputations that affect all immigrant groups. There are always some people who cannot see that gang violence is the work of a select few, and thus assume that all immigrants are part of a larger problem.

learly, Central American immigrants face many challenges. But despite these challenges, there are some success stories. As we stated in chapter 1, America is a nation of immigrants, and each immigrant group makes valuable contributions to this nation as a whole. Central American immigrants are doing their part to make the United States and the world a better place.

ᚺabla ᛖspañol

la situación (lah see-too-ah-see-own): the situation

clinica (clee-nee-kah): clinic

personas (pair-sone-ahs): persons

luchas (loo-chahs): fights, struggles

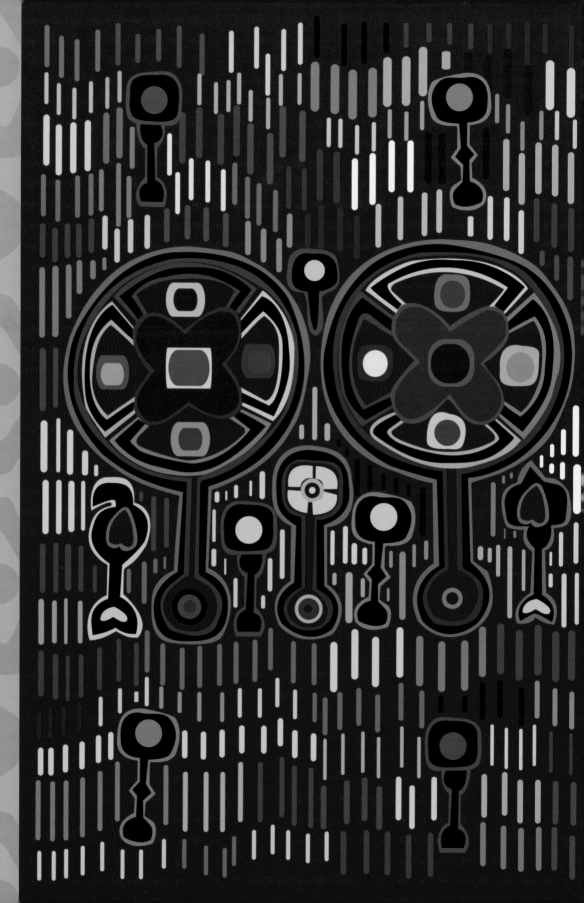

Central Americans Changing Our World

Oscar Arias Sanchez is a former president of Costa Rica, but the impact of his work extends far beyond the boundaries of this country. The Arias Peace Plan, signed by the leaders of five Central American countries in 1987, helped pave the way for a generally peaceful transition to democracy for the region.

Born on September 13, 1941, Arias came from a relatively privileged background, but at an early age he expressed an interest in social justice. While studying at the University of Costa Rica, Arias became active in the National Liberation Party. After receiving his bachelor's degree in 1966, Arias enrolled in the London School of Economics and the University of Essex. His graduate thesis *Who Governs Costa Rica?* was published in 1971.

"Understand that by fighting for the impossible, one begins to make it possible. In that way, no matter how difficult the task, one will never give up. And it doesn't matter if they call us dreamers, idealists. I always said I would rather be don Quixote than to be Pancho. Understand that the idealists of today will be the leaders of tomorrow. And we can't stop dreaming."

—Oscar Arias Sanchez

After working first as a university professor and then in Costa Rica's government, Arias decided to run for President. The theme of his 1984 campaign was simple, direct, and based on the country's most basic needs: "roofs, jobs, and peace." Arias won the election narrowly and took office in 1986. While President he fought for more even distribution of wealth throughout the country and better government. Arias gained a reputation as a politician who cared about the needs of common people, but he did not bind himself with rigid *ideologies* the way many *populist* leaders in the region did. Much of his work focused on bringing peace to Central America, which was then rocked by revolutionary and counter-revolutionary violence. His work in diplomacy gained the notice of the Nobel Prize Committee, which awarded him the 1987 Nobel Peace Prize.

Since leaving the presidency in 1990, Arias took a visiting professorship at Harvard University, where he has written on international affairs and crisis resolution. He has also directed the Arias Foundation, which runs programs on eliminating sexual discrimination, promoting democratic participation, demilitarization, and conflict prevention. Oscar

Arias Sanchez is truly a leader who has changed not only his own country but the world.

Ruben Blades

Ruben Blades freely admits his disdain for boundaries. His career is evidence of this attitude. After beginning his adult life as a bank lawyer, Blades became famous as a musician. Later, he earned a master's degree in international law from Harvard, entered politics in his native Panama, and began acting in films.

Blades was born July 16, 1948, the son of two nightclub musicians. While the family was poor financially, it was rich with the love of music, and Blades as a youngster wanted to become a musician. His father, who was also a police officer, insisted that Blades attend college and study law. When Blades visited the United States after college, however, he became interested in salsa music. He signed a contract with a record label and in 1978 recorded a best-selling salsa album.

Blades' music was different from that of many other artists because of its political edge. He didn't just write about love; he also sang about social issues. For example, his song "*Tiburon*" (Shark) criticized superpowers like the United States for bullying smaller countries.

As the popularity of his music grew, Blades became a leader in the *Nueva Cancion* movement, a musical movement in Latin America that blended protest politics and poetry with traditional folk music. In 1984, Blades became the first Latino artist

ideologies: organized systems of beliefs, values, and ideas forming the basis of a social, economic, or political program.

populist: someone who emphasizes ordinary people.

to sign with a major record label when he began recording with Elektra/Asylum. Over the years, he has won two Grammy awards and recorded with artists such as Linda Ronstadt and Joe Jackson. In 1988, he released a record in English titled *Nothing but the Truth*.

In the mid-1980s, Blades took some time off from the music business to go back to school, earning his degree from Harvard. He also starred in his first film, *Crossover Dreams*, in 1985.

After Panamanian President Manuel Noriega was ousted by a U.S. invasion in 1989, Blades helped found a political party called *Papa Egoro*. While at first he was noncommittal about running for President, in 1993 he decided to seek the nation's top political post. Despite leading in early presidential polls, when the ballots were tallied Blades came in second with roughly one-quarter of the votes.

Blades returned to the United States, where he has resumed his career. His next role was on Broadway, where he starred in a musical about a Puerto Rican gang member. Through his work, both musical and political, Blades has succeeded in educating people in the United States and in Latin America about the struggles Latin America faces.

Hilda Solis

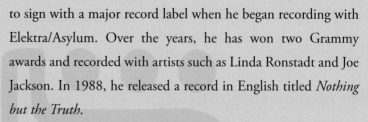he Los Angeles that Hilda Solis experiences every day is a far cry from the glitzy homes of movie stars. Elected in 2000 to represent the 32nd Congressional District of California, Solis comes from a district that is 65 percent Latino

The landfill in Solis's district causes problems for residents.

and 25 percent Asian. It's an area that suffers from polluted water, a shortage of afford-able housing, and smog. Her district includes the largest landfill west of the Mississippi.

Understandably, Solis has pushed for greater assistance from the federal government to poor communities like the one she represents.

"We can demand cleanup, we can demand clean water. Let's unite and see that our community has the same crack at those federal funds just like any other community," she says.

The daughter of a Nicaraguan mother and Mexican father, Solis was the first in her family to graduate from college, earning her bachelor's degree from California State Polytechnic University in 1979 and a master's degree in public administration from the

Low-income families often bear the brunt of pollution's effects.

University of Southern California in 1981. Solis served in the White House Office of Hispanic Affairs during the Carter administration and later worked as an analyst at the Office of Management and Budget.

Solis's first elected position was a seat on the Rio Hondo Community College Board of Trustees in 1985. Later, she served in the California State Assembly from 1992 to 1994, and in 1995 she became the first Latina elected to the State Senate. Solis led efforts to increase the minimum wage in California from $4.25 to $5.75. The increase was vetoed twice by then-Governor Pete Wilson, but it passed as a ballot initiative in 1996.

In August 2000, Solis was the first woman to receive the John F. Kennedy Profile in Courage Award, which recognized her efforts on environmental issues. As a state senator,

Solis worked on legislation that aimed to improve conditions in the low-income and minority communities most affected by pollution and waste.

Solis has lived in the San Gabriel Valley all her life and currently resides in the city of El Monte with her husband.

Michael Cordua

Michael Cordua acquired his cooking skills early. As one of eight children, he took on the chores of preparing food for the family, learning recipes from his mother and from the family's cook. A culinary career, however, was not in the cards at first. A native of Managua, Nicaragua, Cordua earned a degree in economics and finance in 1980 from Texas A&M University, and for several years was a businessperson. In 1987, however, he sold his interest in a shipping business and decided to make his culinary skills into a new career.

Cordua was inspired by a restaurant run by his uncle in Managua, and designed Churrascos, a restaurant that would mix the flavors of Latin American cuisine with North American ingredients. Churrascos opened in August 1988 as the first upscale restaurant in Houston, Texas, specializing in South American cuisine. Two years later, Cordua opened another Churrascos in a different section of the city.

In 1993, Cordua opened Americas, which specialized in the foods of all the Americas—North, Central, and South. Americas was named "Restaurant of the Year" in the November 1993 issue of *Esquire* magazine. The following year, Cordua was named by *Food and Wine* magazine as one of the "Ten Best New Chefs" in the United States. He also received the 1994 Robert Mondavi Award for Culinary Excellence and was a finalist for the 1994 Entrepreneur of the Year award in Houston.

Cordua is active outside the boardroom and the kitchen, too. He chose the *Casa de Esperanza* (House of Hope), a nonprofit crisis center for HIV-positive children, as the beneficiary of charity parties held at his restaurants. More than $500,000 has been raised from these events. Through his culinary skills and his generosity, Michael Cordua is doing much to improve the lives of others. His restaurants share Latin American cuisine and culture with people from all different backgrounds, and his generosity gives hope to those who need it most.

Juan Romagoza

he fact that Juan Romagoza survived a torture chamber in El Salvador is not that unusual. Doctors at the clinic he directs in Washington, D.C., see similar torture survivors every day. What is unusual is that Romagoza successfully sued his torturers in a U.S. courtroom, setting a precedent for other torture victims and making torturers think twice about choosing the United States as a refuge.

Romagoza was a twenty-nine-year-old doctor, part of a team providing free medical care to peasants in the town of Santa Anita, El Salvador, on December 12, 1980, when National Guardsmen attacked, firing machine guns into

Romagoza was arrested because of his shoes!

the crowds of people waiting for medical help. Guardsmen wounded and seized Romagoza. Because he had good hiking shoes, they suspected he was a guerrilla commander. The guardsmen took him to their garrison at El Paraiso.

For twenty-four days, Romagoza was tortured mercilessly. He suffered severe beatings and electric shocks. He was hung by his hands and sometimes by his legs. Romagoza's torturers then shot him through his left arm, taunting him that he would never be able to practice medicine again. Finally, they put him in a coffin barely large enough for his body and kept him there for two days.

Despite the torture Romagoza experienced, he was lucky for eventually he was released, probably through the intervention of two uncles who held high rank in the military. Romagoza's condition was now desperate, but he could not take refuge with friends or family; they were afraid of the consequences. He had to leave El Salvador, fleeing first to Mexico City. He worked there for two years before traveling on to California. In San Francisco, the former doctor worked as a janitor. Despite the fact that he had not yet obtained legal status, Romagoza became active in the movement to make Americans aware of their government's support of brutal governments like El Salvador's. He was at a conference on the issue in Washington in 1986 when he came across La Clinica del Pueblo, which treated the large Latino community in Washington, D.C. He decided to stay on at the clinic as a volunteer.

"Justice for all" requires dedicated individuals like Romagoza.

When the Center for Justice and Accountability contacted Romagoza in 1998, he had become the director of the medical clinic. A lawyer at the center who was an old friend wanted Romagoza to join in a civil lawsuit against two of the men responsible for torturing him—General Jose Garcia and General Carlos Vides Casanova. While many Salvadoran refugees such as Romagoza were forced to enter the United States illegally, the two generals received U.S. visas in 1989 after retiring from the military.

Garcia had been defense minister of El Salvador from 1979 to 1983. Casanova had been head of the National Guard and succeeded Garcia as defense minister. Both men had received commendations from the U.S. government. President Ronald Reagan had given Garcia the U.S. Legion of Merit in 1983. Reagan's secretary of defense had commended Casanova for his "high professional and ethical standards."

When the lawyer proposed suing the two men, Romagoza agreed, but later he had second thoughts. Family members advised him against getting involved. Nevertheless, Romagoza felt an obligation to the other victims of torture. In June 2002, Romagoza and two other victims finally confronted the generals in a courtroom in West Palm Beach, Florida. When he was called to testify, Romagoza described his torture in detail and how during his detention in the National Guard station he had seen Casanova several times.

The jury believed Romagoza and the other two plaintiffs and awarded the three of them $54.6 million. Clearly, the money was important, but it was not the main objective. The case established legal precedent, the first time that such high-ranking military officers living in the United States were held accountable under the Torture Victim Protection Act. The law, which was signed by President George H. W. Bush in 1992, made the generals responsible for torture if they knew of, or should have known of, the torture and did nothing to stop it.

As of the summer of 2004, the plaintiffs have still not collected the monetary award as the courts continued to hear legal appeals by the generals. Romagoza said it was impossible to know when the appeal process would conclude.

"It is important that we have let people like that know that there is no refuge for them here," said Romagoza.

After his case against the generals, other torture victims were also inspired to challenge their former persecutors in court. The Center for Justice and Accountability is now very busy with potential lawsuits against former military men in Central America who tortured people.

"The fundamental principle is the importance of seeking justice. We must be seeking justice," said Romagoza.

Habla Español

justicia (hoos-tee-see-ah): justice

ley (lay): law

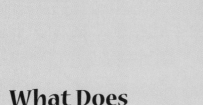

What Does the Future Hold?

A native of El Salvador, Ernesto left in 1981 when the country was increasingly consumed by violence. He says of his experience, "There were many murdered without any reasons. I was really afraid. Two of my cousins and two friends were killed, murdered in 1979, we couldn't believe it. And many acquaintances just disappeared. People were killed by both sides, the death squads and the guerrillas. So one cannot be with one group or with the other; the best thing is to be quiet and not be involved in anything."

A farm in Central America

In the United States, Ernesto worked full time in a restaurant and went to school during the day. Every month, Ernesto sent part of his salary home to his parents. He graduated high school and was accepted to a prestigious university on the West Coast. Ernesto lacked sufficient money to start school, however, so he continued to work through the autumn. By winter, he had saved enough money to start school.

"Now, I will really be able to help my family," Ernesto said.

Despite the great adversity and tragedies many Central Americans have faced, immigrants like Ernesto continue to look to the United States with hope and optimism. Happily, within the United States, many do achieve great success and, like those people we discussed in chapter 5, are able to make significant contributions to their communities and to the world. Unfortunately, the problems confronting Central American immigrants in the years ahead will continue to be many. Economic instability and violence will continue to drive immigrants north, at least for the foreseeable future, and once arriving in the United States, immigrants will continue to struggle as they adjust to a new land, customs, language, and way of life.

Many people feel that the answer to Central Americans' hardships is not making immigration to the United States easier. Rather, the answer is in improving conditions within Central America so that people are no longer forced to emigrate. How to do this, however, is hotly debated, and there are no easy answers.

Free Trade or Fair Trade?

The United States has long been the most influential outside power on Central America, and some people believe economic stability will only arrive in the region through U.S. intervention. Currently, the most hotly debated plan is the setting up of a "free trade zone" with Central America, similar to the free trade zone established within North America under the North American Free Trade Agreement (NAFTA). One of the things the Central American Free Trade Agreement (CAFTA) would do is lift tariffs on 80 percent of U.S. exports to Central America, which come to about $9 billion, and phase out the remaining tariffs

subsidized:
contributed money
in partial support of
something.

over ten years. The United States and the trade representatives of five Central American nations signed the agreement in 2004, but at the time of this publication, the agreement had yet to be ratified officially.

While its supporters say CAFTA will create new economic opportunities for the region by promoting open markets, critics argue that CAFTA will hurt the small national economies of Central America, which are still heavily dependent on subsistence agriculture. They fear that under CAFTA, Central American farmers will be competing against highly **subsidized** production in the United States and elsewhere in the developed world. The prices they will be able to ask for their crops, therefore, will drop. In Mexico, for example, the real price paid to corn farmers fell by roughly 45 percent after NAFTA was enacted. Critics argue that if Central American farmers experience what Mexican farmers experienced, rural poverty will increase and even more people will emigrate. Critics also charge that CAFTA has weak labor and environmental standards, which may allow American companies to take advantage of Central American workers and natural resources. Furthermore, like the earlier NAFTA, CAFTA would establish "corporate rights," allowing corporations and investors to sue governments in secret courts. Some worry that such arrangements take power away from governments, decrease governments' abilities to regulate the way businesses operate, and give businesses special privileges under the law.

In Central America, protests drawing nearly 100,000 people have opposed CAFTA. In the United States, coalitions of human rights, labor, and religious groups have united to protest the lack of an open negotiation process. They're worried that CAFTA will harm, rather than help, the causes of human rights, development, and democracy in Central America.

e do not want immigration to be the only option for our people. We dream of a Central America that provides dignified opportunities that allow them to stay in their communities. Unfortunately, CAFTA will take us farther from that dream.

—Oscar Chacon,
director of Enlaces América's Heartland Alliance

Changing Relationships

o matter what the future brings, one thing is for certain: Central American immigrants will continue to maintain strong connections to their home countries and families abroad. In many cases, these immigrants are still a vital part of the economies of Central American nations for each year they send huge amounts of money to their families back home. Some Central American immigrants also hope to return to Central America one day. Often the decision to immigrate was forced on people by violence and hardship. If they had a choice, they would have stayed with their families in the homes that they loved. Now, as they look toward the future, they hope that improvements in Central America will allow them to return to their homelands.

Home may not be an option for some Central Americans. Many rely on their faith for their sense of stability.

At the same time that some Central American immigrants dream of returning home, however, many others have wholeheartedly embraced life in America. Here they are working, contributing to their communities, raising families, and doing what immigrants have always done—adding to the diversity that makes the United States unique in the world. As part of the Hispanic and Latino communities, Central Americans are becoming ever more visible, and they are changing the face of America in ways both big and small.

 **Habla Español**

futura (foo-too-rah): future

vida (vee-dah): life

Timeline

1502—Christopher Columbus sails into the Bay of Honduras.

1517—Francisco Hernández de Córdoba sails along the coast of Yucatan.

1521—Hernán Cortés overpowers the Aztecs and conquers the city of Tenochtitlan.

September 15, 1821—Central America wins its independence from the Spanish crown.

1823—Guatemala, El Salvador, Honduras, Nicaragua, and Costa Rica form a federation called the United Provinces of Central America.

1984—Ruben Blades becomes the first Latino to sign with a major recording label.

1987—President Oscar Arias Sanchez of Costa Rica wins the Nobel Peace Prize.

1992—President George H. W. Bush signs the Torture Victim Protection Act, allowing for military accountability for torture.

1995—Hilda Solis becomes the first Latina elected to the California State Senate.

August 2000—Hilda Solis becomes the first woman to receive the John F. Kennedy Profiles in Courage Award.

May 28, 2004—The United States, Costa Rica, El Salvador, Guatemala, Honduras, and Nicaragua sign the Central American Free Trade Agreement.

Further Reading

Barry, Tom. *Central America Inside Out: The Essential Guide to Its Societies, Politics and Economics*. New York: Grove Weidenfeld, 1991.

Barry, Tom, Beth Wood, and Deb Preusch. *Dollars & Dictators: A Guide to Central America*. New York: Grove Press, 1983.

Bean, Frank, Jurgen Schmandt, and Sidney Weintraub, eds. *Mexican and Central American Population and U.S. Immigration Policy*. Austin: University of Texas Press, 1989.

Crittenden, Ann. *Sanctuary*. New York: Weidenfeld & Nicolson, 1988.

Foster, Lynn. *A Brief History of Central America*. New York: Facts On File, 2000.

Golden, Renny and Michael McConnel. *Sanctuary: The New Underground Railroad*. Maryknoll, N.Y.: Orbis Books, 1986.

Krauss, Clifford. *Inside Central America: Its People, Politics, and History*. New York: Summit Books, 1991.

Landau, Saul. *Guerrilla Wars of Central America*. New York: St. Martin's Press, 1983.

MacEoin, Gary, ed. *Sanctuary: A Resource Guide for Understanding and Participating in the Central American Refugees' Struggle*. San Francisco: Harper & Row, 1985.

Perez-Brignoli, Hector. *A Brief History of Central America*. Berkeley: University of California Press, 1989.

Suarez-Orozco, Marcelo M. *Central American Refugees and U.S. High Schools: A Psychosocial Study of Motivation and Achievement*. Stanford, Calif.: Stanford University Press, 1989.

For More Information

Central America Daily
www.centralamericadaily.com

Micasa-sucasa
www.ilw.com/micasa/home.htm

The Central American Refugee Center
(Carecen)
www.carecen-la.org

National Immigration Law Center
www.nilc.org/nilcinfo

National Network for Immigrant and
Refugee Rights
www.nnirr.org/

Centralamerica.com
www.centralamerica.com

Enlaces América
www.enlacesamerica.org

Political Resources
www.politicalresources.net/c_amer.htm

The Guatemala Human Rights
Commission
www.ghrc-usa.org

The Washington Office on Latin America
www.wola.org

Hispanic Online
www. hispaniconline.com

Publisher's note:
The Web sites listed on this page were active at the time of publication. The
publisher is not responsible for Web sites that have changed their addresses or
discontinued operation since the date of publication. The publisher will review
and update the Web site list upon each reprint.

Index

Picture Credits

Benjamin Stewart: pp. 55, 56, 69, 71, 75

Carin Zissis, carinzissis@hotmail.com: pp. 44, 52, 62

Corbis: p. 99

Corel: pp. 9, 12, 15, 16, 17, 18, 21, 24, 31, 32, 35, 41, 42, 47, 48, 49, 51, 53, 60, 80, 103, 105

Dianne Hodack: p. 6

Hemera Images: pp. 11, 68, 73, 78, 84

Hollingsworth Studios: pp. 65, 87

Michelle Bouch: pp. 8, 30, 46, 64, 86, 98

Photos.com: pp. 23, 91, 92, 95, 96

PhotoDisc: p. 59

Viola Ruelke Gommer: pp. 66, 72, 76, 100

To the best knowledge of the publisher, all other images are in the public domain. If any image has been inadvertently uncredited, please notify Harding House Publishing Service, Vestal, New York 13850, so that rectification can be made for future printings.

Biographies

Eric Schwartz is a journalist living in Binghamton, New York. He received his bachelor's degree in Russian and journalism from Michigan State University and his master's degree in international relations from Syracuse University.

Dr. José E. Limón is professor of Mexican-American Studies at the University of Texas at Austin where he has taught for twenty-five years. He has authored over forty articles and three books on Latino cultural studies and history. He lectures widely to academic audiences, civic groups, and K–12 educators.